Courage

A JOURNAL TO EXPLORE YOUR BOLD, BRAVE SPIRIT

Katie Caples

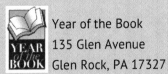

Year of the Book

135 Glen Avenue

Glen Rock, PA 17327

ISBN 13: 978-1-949150-31-5

ISBN 10: 1-949150-31-3

INTRODUCTION

Courage is a choice and is something we often admire in others. We all possess courage, and for many of us it is at its peak during our earliest years. My braver, fiercer self just so happened to be a bold child who jumped from things far too high, dove into mud, sand and dirt, and enthusiastically pushed the bounds of each new thing tried.

I remember well the days of my childhood... playing spaceship with my sister by climbing the tallest, sappiest pine in our backyard forest; swimming beyond the buoys in the cold, murky lake nestled in the heart of my hometown; and riding our horses bareback with little more than a halter, the mountains as our backdrop.

I hope you have fond memories, too. As you reflect on your many adventures, you may find yourself asking... when did my courageous spirit start to dull? If so, this journal is for you.

As you open your heart to reconnect with your bold, brave spirit, this journal will both encourage and challenge you. Embrace it is a list keeper, doodle book, spiritual map, or reflective guide. Start at the beginning or flip to a random page that speaks to your heart.

I invite you to slow down, create space and nurture your courageous voice as you explore your narrative.

To you, with love.

OWNING OUR STORY
AND LOVING OURSELVES
THROUGH THAT PROCESS
IS THE BRAVEST THING
THAT WE'LL EVER DO.

-- BRENÉ BROWN

MY MOST PAINFUL CHAPTERS:

WE ARE TENDER AND FIERCE.
WE ARE SOFT AND STRONG.
WE ARE FRAGILE AND COURAGEOUS.
SOMETIMES ALL IN ONE DAY.

-- UNKNOWN

AN EXAMPLE OF HOW I AM...

TENDER:

FIERCE:

SOFT:

STRONG:

FRAGILE:

COURAGEOUS:

With courage
you will dare
to take risks,
have the strength
to be compassionate,
and the wisdom
to be humble.

-- Mark Twain

I AM STRONG BECAUSE:

I AM WISE WHEN:

STORMS MAKE TREES
TAKE DEEPER ROOTS.

-- DOLLY PARTON

MY ROOTS, MY FOUNDATION...

- ○
- ○
- ○
- ○
- ○

It takes courage
to grow up and be
who you really are.

-- E.E. Cummings

WHEN I GROW UP, I WILL BE:

All our dreams can come true
if we have the courage
to pursue them.

-- Walt Disney

MY DREAMS:

One of the most
courageous
decisions you'll
ever make is to
finally let go
of what is hurting
your heart and soul.

-- Brigette Nicole

I CHOOSE TO LET GO OF...

HAVE THE COURAGE
TO FOLLOW YOUR
HEART AND INTUITION.
THEY SOMEHOW KNOW
WHAT YOU TRULY WANT
TO BECOME.

-- STEVE JOBS

MY HEART AND INTUITION TELL ME TO:

SAVOR WHAT YOU ARE AND
NOT WHAT EVERYONE ELSE
WANTS YOU TO BE.

-- SANDRA BULLOCK

THINGS I SAVOR:

1

2

3

ONLY IN THE DARKNESS
CAN YOU SEE THE STARS.

-- MARTIN LUTHER KING JR.

STARS IN MY LIFE:

LIFE IS EITHER
A DARING ADVENTURE
OR NOTHING AT ALL.

-- HELEN KELLER

MY DARING ADVENTURES:

Courage doesn't always roar.
Sometimes courage is the quiet
voice at the end of the day saying,
'I will try again tomorrow.'

-- MaryAnne Radmacher

THINGS I WILL TRY AGAIN...

O

O

O

O

STRENGTH DOES NOT
COME FROM WINNING.

YOUR STRUGGLES
DEVELOP YOUR
STRENGTHS.

WHEN YOU GO THROUGH
HARDSHIPS AND DECIDE
NOT TO SURRENDER,
THAT IS STRENGTH.

-- MAHATMA GANDHI

A SNAPSHOT OF MY JOURNEY...

Hardships endured:	Strengths as a result:

You Have To Believe
In yourself when
no one else Does.

-- serena williams

I BELIEVE I AM...

Every great dream
begins with a
dreamer.

-- Harriet Tubman

MY BIGGEST, SCARIEST DREAM:

If you want your life to go
beyond ordinary to
extraordinary,
you must expand
your concept of yourself.

To reach extraordinary levels,
where all things are possible,
you must change what you
believe is true about yourself.

-- Wayne Dyer

BELIEFS I WILL CHANGE...

Do one thing every day that scares you.

-- Eleanor Roosevelt

MY TO-DO'S...

Today's scary thing:

Tomorrow's scary thing:

YOU WERE MADE FOR MORE
THAN YOU EVEN KNOW.

YOU WERE MADE FOR MORE
THAN THIS.

STOP STALLING, START RUNNING.

-- REBECCA COOPER

I AM RUNNING TOWARDS...

1

2

3

IT ALWAYS SEEMS
IMPOSSIBLE
UNTIL IT'S DONE.

-- NELSON MANDELA

IN 5 YEARS, I WILL PROUDLY SAY...

LIFE IS...
10% WHAT HAPPENS TO YOU
AND
90% HOW YOU REACT TO IT.

-- CHARLES R. SWINDOLL

HARD MOMENTS IN MY LIFE...

THINGS THAT HAPPENED: MY REACTION:

YOU CAN'T PUT A LIMIT ON ANYTHING.
THE MORE YOU DREAM,
THE FARTHER YOU GET.

-- MICHAEL PHELPS

LIMITS (LIES) THAT I TELL MYSELF:

HERE'S WHAT I THINK INTEGRITY IS:
IT'S CHOOSING COURAGE OVER COMFORT.
CHOOSING WHAT'S RIGHT OVER WHAT'S
FUN, FAST OR EASY.

AND PRACTICING YOUR VALUES.

- - BRENÉ BROWN

MY CORE VALUES:

○

○

○

○

○

GROWTH ALMOST ALWAYS
HAPPENS OUTSIDE YOUR
COMFORT ZONE.

-- KERRI WALSH-JENNINGS

AREAS I'D LIKE TO GROW:

BELIEVE IN THE
BEAUTY OF YOUR
HEART'S WISHES.

-- AUDREY HEPBURN

MY HEART'S WISHES...

Pain can change you,
but that doesn't mean it
has to be a bad change.

Take that pain and turn
it into wisdom.

-- Dalai Lama

BITS OF WISDOM GAINED:

The universe is full
of magic things,
patiently waiting for our
senses to become sharper.

-- Eden Phillpotts

MAGICAL THINGS I SEE:

1

2

3

4

5

I can shake off
everything as I write;
my sorrows disappear,
my courage is reborn.

-- Anne Frank

THINGS I WISH TO SHAKE OFF...

•••

A QUIET MIND
IS ABLE TO HEAR
INTUITION OVER FEAR.

-- UNKNOWN

•••

I QUIET MY MIND BY:

•••

•••

•••

patience is the calm acceptance
that things can happen
in a different order
than the one you have in mind.

--David G. Allen

I AM CALMLY ACCEPTING...

close your eyes and
imagine the best version
of you possible.

that's who you really are,

let go of any part of you
that doesn't believe it.

-- C. ASSaaD

I RELEASE...

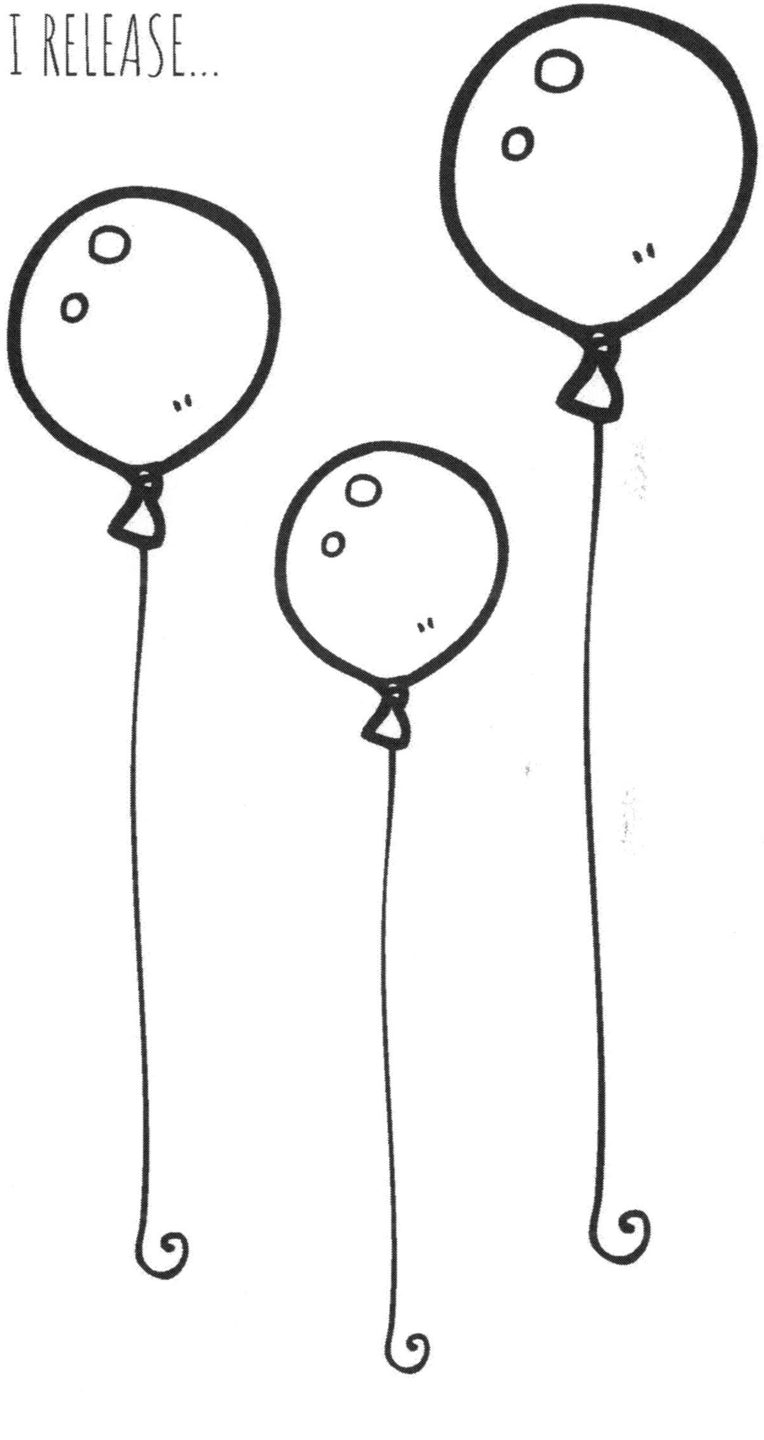

THE WORLD WILL SEE YOU
THE WAY YOU SEE YOU.

-- BEYONCÉ KNOWLES

WHEN I LOOK IN THE MIRROR, I SEE...

The storm can be just as beautiful as the rainbow, honor them both.

-- Alex Elle

THE STORMS THAT I HONOR:

THE RAINBOWS THAT I HONOR:

May my heart be kind,
my mind fierce,
and my spirit brave.

-- Kate Forsyth

TODAY, MY HEART IS...

MY MIND IS...

MY SPIRIT IS...

A HERO:
IS AN ORDINARY
INDIVIDUAL WHO FINDS
THE STRENGTH TO
PERSEVERE AND ENDURE
IN SPITE OF
OVERWHELMING OBSTACLES.

-- CHRISTOPHER REEVE

MY HEROES (AND WHY):

NEVERTHELESS, SHE PERSISTED.

-- UNKNOWN

THE REASONS I PERSIST...

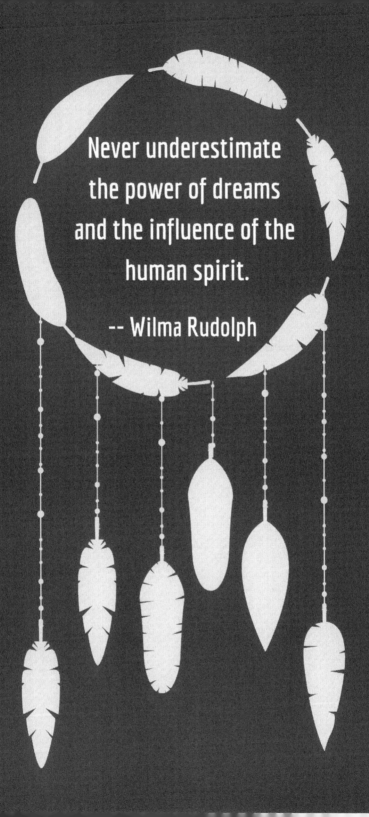

Never underestimate the power of dreams and the influence of the human spirit.

-- Wilma Rudolph

MY EARLIEST CHILDHOOD DREAMS:

Do not let the
behavior of others
destroy your
inner peace.

-- Dalai Lama

PEOPLE WHO NEGATIVELY AFFECT ME...

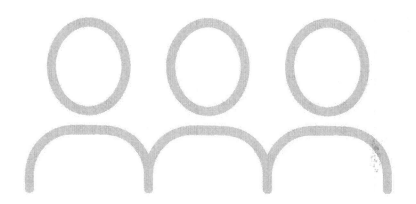

THEY TRIGGER ME BECAUSE...

Always remember
you have within you
the strength,
the patience
and the passion
to reach for the stars
to change the world.

-- Harriet Tubman

MY STRENGTHS...

MY PASSIONS...

MY WORLD...

COURAGE IS NOTHING MORE
THAN TAKING ONE STEP MORE THAN
YOU THINK YOU CAN.

-- HOLLY LISLE

MY MOST COURAGEOUS STEPS...

There's only one
thing more precious
than our time and
that's WHO we
spend it on.

-- Leo Christopher

WHAT I SPEND MY TIME ON:

WHO I SPEND MY TIME ON:

YOU DON'T HAVE TO
SEE THE WHOLE STAIRCASE,
JUST TAKE THE FIRST STEP.

-- MARTIN LUTHER KING JR.

MY NEXT STEPS...

1

2

3

THERE IS BEAUTY IN EVERYTHING. EVEN IN SILENCE AND DARKNESS.

-- HELEN KELLER

THE DARKNESS IN MY LIFE:

O

O

O

O

O

The most effective
way to do it,
is to do it.

-- Amelia Earhart

I THRIVE WHEN...

It takes as much
energy to *wish*
as it does to *plan*.

-- Eleanor Roosevelt

MY PLANS...

In One Year: | In Ten Years:

She was brave and strong and broken all at once.

-- Anna Funder

I AM BRAVE WHEN:

I AM STRONG BECAUSE:

I AM THE MOST BROKEN:

THE HARDEST STEP
SHE EVER TOOK
WAS TO BLINDLY TRUST
IN WHO SHE WAS.

-- ATTICUS

THINGS I KNOW TO BE TRUE...

•••

LIFE SHRINKS AND EXPANDS
IN PROPORTION
TO ONE'S COURAGE.

-- ANAÏS NIN

WAYS I WILL EXPAND MY LIFE:

●●●

●●●

●●●

It is ok to be scared.
Being scared means
you're about to do
something really,
really brave.

-- Unknown

MY SCARIEST MOMENTS:

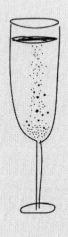

The way you think
determines the way you feel,
and the way you feel determines
the way you act.

-- T.K. Makhura

TODAY, I'M FEELING...

Travel light.
Live light.
Be the light.
Spread the light.

-- Unknown

WAYS IN WHICH I SPREAD LIGHT:

- ○
- ○
- ○
- ○
- ○

EACH TIME
WE FACE OUR FEAR,
WE GAIN STRENGTH,
COURAGE, AND CONFIDENCE
IN THE DOING.

-- THEODORE ROOSEVELT

I AM MOST CONFIDENT WHEN...

LIFE IS
BETTER
WHEN I
REMEMBER
THAT I'M
STRONG,
RESILIENT,
CAPABLE,
AND GIFTED.

-- UNKNOWN

LIFE IS BETTER WITH...

My Strengths:

My Gifts:

YOU GET IN LIFE
WHAT YOU HAVE THE
COURAGE TO ASK FOR.

-- OPRAH WINFREY

MY BIGGEST, BOLDEST FUTURE ASKS...

1

2

3

I've found that the changes I feared would ruin me have always become doorways, and on the other side I have found a more courageous and graceful self.

-- Elizabeth Lesser

POSITIVE WORDS THAT DESCRIBE ME:

Don't be pushed
by your problems.
Be led by your dreams.

-- Ralph Waldo Emerson

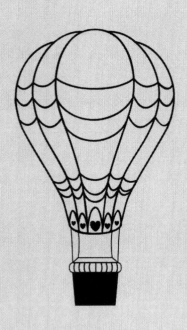

PROBLEMS THAT PUSH ME:

DREAMS THAT LEAD ME:

TO LIVE A CREATIVE LIFE,
WE MUST LOSE OUR FEAR
OF BEING WRONG.

-- JOSEPH CHILTON PEARCE

I FEAR...

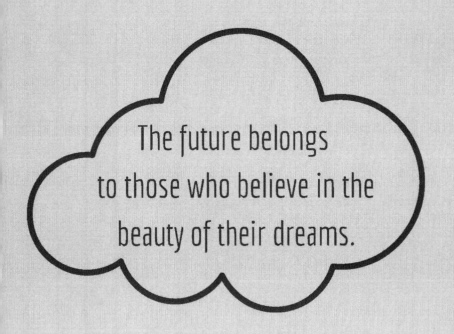

The future belongs
to those who believe in the
beauty of their dreams.

-- Eleanor Roosevelt

I BELIEVE IN THE BEAUTY OF...

WHEN THE GOING GETS TOUGH,
MAY I CHOOSE LOVE OVER FEAR.
EVERY TIME.

-- KATRINA KENISON

TODAY, I CHOOSE...

MY HOPE
IS THAT YOU
STEP OUTSIDE
OF THE COMFORT
OF YOUR BOXES AND
WHOLLY AND BOLDLY
BE YOUR TRUEST,
FIERCEST SELF.

-- JANET MOCK

MY TRUEST, FIERCEST SELF WOULD...

In the end, only three things matter:
how much you loved,
how gently you lived, and
how gracefully you let go of things
not meant for you.

-- Buddha

HOW MUCH I LOVE:

HOW GENTLY I LIVE:

HOW GRACEFULLY I LET GO OF THINGS:

ACKNOWLEDGMENTS

Many amazing people have nurtured my courageous spirit.

A special shout out to:

My paternal grandmother, Phyllis. Faced with a terminal diagnosis of glioblastoma, an aggressive form of brain cancer, she stood strong in her faith and cherished her family and friends. Gram was the kindest person I have ever known. Her love and grace will forever live on in the hearts of the generations that follow. A beautiful, brave soul.

My daughters, Addison and Lauren. Your adventurous spirits and sense of wonder fill my heart with joy; you inspire me every day. Mama loves you through and through.

ABOUT THE AUTHOR

Katie Caples is a doer, dreamer and entrepreneur. She's a wife and mom of two beautiful daughters. A farm girl from the mountains of western Maryland, Katie lives with her family in Stewartstown, Pennsylvania, along with steers, horses, chickens and her trusty dog, Cosmo. She practices gratitude and takes time to enjoy the simple things.

Her intent with this journal is space – space to explore your inner thoughts and cultivate your courageous voice. As Katie found inspiration in writing and publishing her first book, *Clarity: A Journal for Reflection & Discovery*, she took to journaling to continue to grow and expand her life. With a brave heart, she transitioned from her beloved nonprofit career to raise her children, launch her business and pursue her passions of writing and journaling.

To join Katie on her journey, visit her at kcaples.com.

Made in the USA
Middletown, DE
26 November 2018